Through the Eyes

DATE DUE	RETURNED

DON DRUICK

(60201)

Through the Eyes

LIVRES
DC
BOOKS

Cover illustration by Normand Cousineau.
Book designed and typeset in Adobe Garamond Pro
and Myriad MM by Primeau & Barey, Montreal.

Printed and bound in Canada by AGMV Marquis.
Distributed by Lit DistCo.

Legal Deposit, Bibliothèque nationale du Québec
and the National Library of Canada, 4th trimester, 2004.

Library and Archives Canada Cataloguing in Publication
Druick, Don, 1945–
Through the eyes / Don Druick.

ISBN 0-919688-15-2
1. Title.
PS8557.R78T47 2004 C812'.54 C2004-906143-7

DC Books gratefully acknowledges the support
of The Canada Council for the Arts, The Book
Publishing Industry Development Program
of the Department of Canadian Heritage, and
of SODEC for our publishing program.

 Canada Council   Conseil des Arts
for the Arts   du Canada

Société
de développement
des entreprises
culturelles
Québec 🔲🔲
           🔲🔲

DC Books
950 Decarie, Box 662
Montreal, Quebec, H4L 4V9
www.dcbooks.ca

*To Brian Quirt, for sharing
my passion for* Through the Eyes
*and for giving this play voice
so many times in so many ways.*

Foreword

Through the Eyes or *Bernini Bernana Bernono*

The writing of every play is a personal odyssey, an inquiry into representation, expression, and desire. Difficult and exhilarating. For as my Gianlorenzo Bernini says: "the disappointment of expectations makes us foreign to our own universe.... Another constant battle."

The story: Gianlorenzo Bernini comes to France, 1665.

I started writing *Through the Eyes* in 1992 while in Tokyo, the first draft in ten days. Originally, a research offshoot of my *Barocco Romano,* in which there is yet another quite different Bernini character, *Through the Eyes* has acquired its very own and special patina of baroque experience, which, truth be known, is my favourite.

Through the Eyes is told to us by the Courtier. All the other voices that we hear, some frequently, some only once, are related by him, through him. Anonymous, the journey of the play is finally his, for we see what he sees, and we sense what he feels. And in discovering him, as he discovers himself, we are made aware of an as yet unknown center of our own universe.

And why Bernini? Because as the definitive artist of the 17th century, as the creator of exquisite form and beauty, as perhaps the most celebrated and prosperous artist of all time, as the master of the total environment, Bernini becomes a model for what an artist can be. He is our filter, our cypher for the past. He also becomes that part of all of us which moves mountains in our dreams.

I would like very much to thank for their generous, insightful discourse and support: Brian Quirt, Jane Buyers, Naomi Campbell, Patrick Conner, Michael Devine, Zoë Druick, Peter Hinton, Jeannette Lambermont, Mollye Reisler, Julian Richings, Michael Rudder, Renée Tannenbaum, Emmanuelle Roy, Vera Golini, Richard McMillan, and The Canada Council, Canadian Stage Company, Nightswimming Theatre, Factory Theatre, and Playwrights Workshop Montreal.

Don Druick
Elmira

Through the Eyes is a play for one actor, performing the following characters (in order of appearance).

THE COURTIER, our narrator
LOUIS XIV, the King of France
PIERRE CLAUDE-MARIE LAROCHE, the Master of the Hunt
THE MARQUIS DE BELLEFONDS, the King's hatchet
CAVALIERE GIANLORENZO BERNINI, the great Italian maestro
CARDINAL ANTONIO BARBERINI, the Papal nuncio
MOLIÈRE, a playwright
MADAME LA PRINCESSE, the Queen's aunt
MARIE-THÉRÈSE, the Queen of France
MADEMOISELLE DE SAINT-CHRISTOPHE, a lady of the court
MONSIEUR WARIN, an artist

The setting is Paris and Versailles, France, 1665.

Over and over again
it is always necessary to keep reminding myself
that I have ever really done anything

–Gianlorenzo Bernini

Act One

COURTIER There is an incident at Fontainebleau. Our master Louis is hunting–is it the falcons or the hounds?–and, and we with him. It is beautiful beautiful an early spring day. How I love these days, the buds the air, crisp and clear so clear. One feels for a moment one can really see! We are all in fine fettle, the gentlemen of the court, despite having been up oh so late the night before tasting of the sparkling local vintage. That night, how we did laugh, the King at his wittiest as we sang the old songs of François Villon. So beautiful to remember these soulful melodies. And why? And especially now? Can it be that it is like my childhood?

So as is said, we are hunting but we can find no worthy prey. No brocket no boar nor stag. It is the nature of the game: nothing worthy, nothing… banal… nothing, nothing at all. We search and search we ride we seek but nothing absolutely nothing. After a long while of this, *mon* Louis, the mirror of all our souls, turns suddenly to his Master of the Hunt, his father's Master of the Hunt, Pierre Claude-Marie LaRoche.

AS LOUIS And so, *Monsieur* LaRoche?
AS LAROCHE M'Lord?
AS LOUIS And so?
AS LAROCHE M'Lord?

1

AS LOUIS There is nothing, *Monsieur* LaRoche. What are we to imagine?

AS LAROCHE *Je suis désolé,* M'Lord, but what can one do?

AS LOUIS Is that it then?

AS LAROCHE M'Lord?

AS LOUIS Is that it? Would you have done as little for my father?

AS LAROCHE Old King Louis, m'Lord?

We laugh at poor Pierre's plight. I decide then and there I will give him a bottle of my finest cognac when the day is done. We laugh but something, how shall I convey this, in the King's tone quickly sobers us. *Mon* Louis, our heartbeat, hesitates. The Marquis de Bellefonds, the King's left hand, the Minister Of Culture, and perhaps it is rumored, the Fifth Musketeer, whispers in the royal ear.

AS BELLEFONDS What say you, Sire, should not this LaRoche be our prey?

AS LOUIS Ah. [*Pause*] Yes. So be it.

AS LAROCHE I do not understand, M'Lord.

AS BELLEFONDS Be as a little animal. Go. Run. Scamper!

AS LAROCHE M'Lord?

Monsieur LaRoche is shivering in the morning cold.

AS LOUIS Be off. [*Pause*] Now.

AS BELLEFONDS And without your horse.

In the silence, a bird, suddenly so large, flies across the sky. Pierre turns and runs. We look to the King.

AS LOUIS Give him five, no, ten minutes, and then we pursue. We will have meat for the table tonight, eh?

The laughter that follows is dry, and quickly disappears into the landscape. The silence is long.

AS LOUIS [*Pause*] Now. Loose the hounds. We ride. Which way? Which way? Yes. There. There he is. Towards the palace!

LaRoche is almost at the gates. *Mon* Louis, the regal Louis laughs. The Marquis de Bellefonds cannot resist the opportunity to shout:

AS BELLEFONDS He is looking for a bed to hide under.
AS LOUIS A bag of gold to the man who kills the game.

We enter the palace itself, horses hounds harriers. An awesome sight. Inside the palace inside the very palace. A roar like I have never heard before. By now LaRoche has climbed the grand marble staircase magnificent glistening pure white, the heartbeat of the palace, broad and sweeping up and up and up till it almost touches sweet heaven itself. Our Louis the sailor of all the oceans, charges the staircase his horse slipping and cracking on the marble.

Most follow the King, but I... stay behind. The smell in the air is blood.

AS LOUIS Flourish the mort. Flourish the mort.

The roar the racket a symphony of death. The devil's hounds do howl. LaRoche is almost at the top when the first rider, the Chevalier de Nogent, the youngest son of the legendary Prince de Condé, splendid in a blue damask jacket splendid upon a regal white stallion, reaches him passes him rears above him. The moment is sublime: white horse white marble white eyes. Forever. Suddenly with a swift oh so swift swift motion, the Chevalier de Nogent reaches down with his dagger and cuts Pierre's throat one side to the other. Blood everywhere now, the marble alive with colour. Blue jacket white horse red blood. Pierre Claude-Marie LaRoche with a gargled cry slowly crumbling jerking painfully spasmodically arms legs flailing as he falls tumbling slowly down down down down down accelerating now more and faster faster again and coming to a rest his final rest just two stairs from the bottom. Almost in front of me. At moments like this, I pray: oh Lord, please grant me just one more day on this earth!

AS LOUIS Well there it is.

LaRoche's eyes remain open.

It is our sacred tradition that the royal family may never sleep, will never sleep, in a house where someone has died. So the Marquis de Bellefonds drags the perhaps and barely alive Pierre Claude-Marie LaRoche, a trail of blood, to die alone in the darkening mist of the courtyard. I think of Isabelle, his wife of so many years. I silently vow never to hunt again. I know I will drink that bottle of my finest cognac when the day is done.

The King turns to me.

AS LOUIS And is not *Cavaliere* Berninino arriving at Versailles tomorrow? Certainly there is still much to be arranged.

COURTIER Is it not Bernini, Sire, or so I have been led to believe.

AS LOUIS These Italian names. One can hardly understand the very sounds. *Mon* Condé, where is the Queen? I wish to see her.

⊙

Mon Louis is right, as always. For weeks the talk at the King's *levée* has been of nothing else. Revered in Rome, sculptor architect confidant to the Popes builder of brilliant monuments and palaces, yes, *Cavaliere* Gianlorenzo Bernini now comes to France.

AS LOUIS A royal escort is to be given to the Italian. All is to be a magnificent triumphal procession. Be certain that he is impressed. I cannot believe, *mon* Bellefonds, that Innocenzo could have let such a treasure fall between his fingers. I tell you I cannot believe it.

[*Bellefonds laughs*]

The Marquis de Bellefonds' laugh, as prominent as it can be, is barely heard midst the now more than usual uproar of Versailles. All is abuzz. Chaos barely controlled. It is whispered that *Cavaliere* Bernini is despised by the new Pope, Innocenzo. Our young King, Louis, the fabric of all our dreams, would be preeminent over Austria over Rome and as always, over Spain. Scheming, ruthless Pope Innocenzo blocks him at every pass. It is also whispered that the presence of *Cavaliere* Bernini in Paris will clearly and undeniably demonstrate the truth of France's majesty. All is abuzz in Versailles.

In honour of the Italian's arrival, the court has been instructed to appear in sumptuous new clothing. Therefore a mad desperate I have never ever seen it like this a desperate scramble for tailors dress-makers working frantically feverishly throughout the night. Myself, I will wear *Bleu Poussin*. And such a shade... from old Provençe. All is so abuzz in Versailles.

As I speak a little of the Italian I have been given the task of attending to the *Cavaliere's* needs. It is the very first occasion that I have been graced with a request by my beloved Louis and I cannot refuse him! I now have apartments in Versailles, small ones to be sure and off an irksome noisy corridor but nonetheless in the north wing. One never knows midst the endless rumors and desires and variations of the truth at Versailles where it will all lead. At last a position of quality could be mine. [*Pause*] Then will She be mine?

We arrive early in the morning, I and this Italian artist, for the King will see Bernini at the *levée*. As we approach the Royal apartments the *Cavaliere* remarks on the small golden vessel, a little ship in the center of one of the long succession of silent outer chambers.

COURTIER *Ah, c'est la Nef du Roi. Oui.* Ummm. Ummm. *Tovagliolo.* For cleaning the royal genitalia. [*Pause*] *Organi maschili.* We will have our ways in France, *Cavaliere.* These napkins are, for us, in a sense, the future, and ritual demands that everyone passing *la Nef du Roi* bow. Like this. Let me show you. You are in France now. We are most particular. The left leg thrust forward so. The right knee bent like so. The hat moved like so in a graceful semicircle head to stomach. No no, *Cavaliere,* start with the other leg. You have gotten it backwards. [*Pause*]

I protest, *Cavaliere.*

The next antechamber is small and dim, a single oval window set on high. Here, crushed together, are the most eminent gentlemen in France waiting to greet the glorious Louis.

COURTIER Do you remember the bow?

Could he feel the contempt in my voice?

Our noble King is by the window with the First Gentleman Of The Bedchamber and The Master Of The Wardrobe. There are the gentlemen of the King's family: the *Grand Dauphin,* who is the only legitimate son and a mere child, and the King's brother, *Monsieur,* the Duc d'Orléans. Is it clear that the *Cavaliere* is impressed by the elegance of the room? The King's bed on a dais of red damask behind a gilded wooden balustrade, the corners surmounted by white ostrich plumes and egret feathers like jets of water over breaking waves. A cold light pervades the room, the courtyard below full of mist.

The King prays, his hands are washed in a gold and porcelain cockleshell, he is shaved. His son and brother hold a dressing gown as a screen letting it fall, revealing *mon* Louis drinking his broth. I smile inside. I am in the presence of the King, the spirit of greatness that is France. The father of all brothers. The Master of Ceremonies, the Royal

Butler, the Royal Taster and the man whose function is to hold the plate under the royal chin form a semi-circle about him. *Mon* Louis puts on his coat chooses a cravat handkerchief gloves hat cane. Resting his hand on the jeweled hilt of his sword his other hand idyllic on the knob of his cane, *mon* Louis turns to the *Cavaliere.*

AS LOUIS So now you are in France, *Cavaliere* Bernaizi.

AS BERNINI Bernini, Sire.

AS LOUIS Good, very good.

AS BERNINI Majesty, it is my desire to serve you in all things. I have so many many ideas. I have built the greatest *palazzi* for the glory of the Popes of *Roma....*

COURTIER But for the complete allegiance to the King of France....

AS BERNINI But for the glory of the King of France, a monarch of our own time, there is a need for something still greater and even more magnificent. Your Majesty, I crave to serve you, but I make one request only.

AS LOUIS And that is?

AS BERNINI I beg you: speak to me only of projects not *diminutivo.*

COURTIER "Inconsequential," Sire.

AS LOUIS Yes yes, I know. Exactly, Monsieur. Good. Very good. Now this indeed is the man as I have imagined him. Unlike elsewhere, we truly appreciate you here in France. *Cavaliere,* I have the notion that I will not be able to surpass history. What do you think of this?

AS BERNINI We will see. I will try. You will try.

AS LOUIS Good. Very good. As far as money is concerned there is no need for any restriction. See to it, *mon* Bellefonds.

I had not seen the Marquis de Bellefonds enter. I am becoming careless.

AS BELLEFONDS At once, Majesty.

I am becoming careless. Oh but we live in difficult and dangerous times but who can not say this? The struggle. The journey of my life. I am tired for it. Exhausted with expectations at court frustrations at court despair and lone-liness. In the depths of the night I crave tenderness, a true intimacy.

The noise of the men on the other side of the door is suddenly very loud. It draws me, startles me from my reverie.

AS BERNINI He is a divinely gifted monarch....
COURTIER *Mais certainement.*
AS BERNINI ... with an understanding of art.

I shake my head. Can the *Cavaliere* really be so naive?

We meet Marie-Thérèse, the Queen of France; in attendance, *Madame La Princesse,* the sister of the King of Spain and therefore the Queen's aunt, and the Prince de Condé, the Queen's cousin and her personal emissary to the King's court. Wounded in battle, his horse fell upon him, he now dresses only in ultramarine. The shade has been named after him.

Today, I have bowed, for the first time I have bowed this very day to the Queen of France. She is very kind to the *Cavaliere.* They speak in Italian but rapidly in the Vatican dialect, the language of secrets. It will be better if I do not understand them.

The Marquis de Bellefonds himself, I notice the Queen does not deign to look in his direction, escorts the *Cavaliere* to the Hôtel de Frontenac in Paris where he is to live and work. The *Cavaliere* goes to the chapel where he remains a long time in prayer, prostrate upon the floor, kissing the marble. Kissing the marble.

We meet Cardinal Antonio Barberini, the Papal nuncio. Has this been arranged? Impeccably elegantly dressed in his scarlet robes, speaking slowly, as always, in his deep booming melodious voice, his Eminence has the reputation of one who always achieves his ends. I must be careful. It would not do to be considered too close to the Italians.

AS CARDINAL BARBERINI The Queen of France has spent much time in *Roma,* though I did not know her there of course.

AS BERNINI I had the pleasure of Her Majesty's company in *Roma.*

I cannot think for the horror of what this might mean!

AS CARDINAL BARBERINI Look over there. From this height Paris seems nothing but a mass of chimneys. Like the teeth in a comb

AS BERNINI *Roma* is a very different sight, much more beautiful.

AS CARDINAL BARBERINI Perhaps *Roma* is where you should be, *Cavaliere,* instead of here, among the French.

AS BERNINI The French appreciate me.

⊙

This early spring the daffodils are for me these days suddenly not sufficient. *Je suis tellement triste.*

⊙

He is in his atelier in the Hôtel de Frontenac working on his own self-portrait in red chalk.

AS BERNINI In *Roma* I am in the habit of walking up and down and up and down the *galleria* where I put on the very walls the ideas as they come to me. I miss this.

He becomes very annoyed, suddenly, and stops his work.
I cannot understand it. I wonder what in the work can be
so displeasing to him.

AS BERNINI *Nelle mie opere caco sangue.* What does this
mean? Do you know?

COURTIER "In my work I shed blood."

AS BERNINI *Sì, esattamente.* I have heard from various
sources that the King wants me to make his portrait in
stone. Is this true?

COURTIER The Marquis de Bellefonds has said nothing
about it. Who has told you this?

AS BERNINI The Prince de Condé was kind enough to men-
tion it. Then Cardinal Antonio Barberini.

COURTIER Do you speak often with the Cardinal?

The *Cavaliere* receives so many foreign letters.

AS BERNINI So? Is it true? Does the King wish this?

COURTIER How do I know? I am not party to the intimacies
of the King's mind.

AS BERNINI I will start with a bust and I will need to get
started right away, *à presto,* for it will take me four
months such a commission, and there is more and other
significant work that I wish to do here.

I remain silent.

⊙

In order to keep him amused and placated, I am required to spend many hours in search of a suitable block of marble. The day drags on insufferably. The *Cavaliere* is so particular. The gardens of the Tuileries along the waterside with their celebrated beech and popular trees now gloriously in bloom are so beautiful. To the Val-de-Grâce, where the *Cavaliere* finally chooses, begrudgingly, only three stones [*Imitating Bernini*] perhaps possible to work with. [*As himself*] The costs are sixteen hundred and three *livres.*

AS BERNINI So expensive in France and such poor quality.
COURTIER If you insist, *Cavaliere,* I will write a letter on your behalf to someone, a dealer I have heard of.
AS BERNINI *Grazie.* I must have my marble immediately.

⊙

The *Cavaliere* is invited to the stables at Versailles, a private and select ceremony, to witness the elegant Louis preside over the gelding of the royal stallion, Brutus. The Chevalier de Nogent, splendid in a blue damask jacket, is present, as is his father, the Prince de Condé, and the Marquis de Bellefonds. The great Molière, forever in the Temple of Memory, who is the King's favourite, and mine, regales us.

AS MOLIÈRE *De non jamais te servire*
De remediis aucunis....

Maladus dût-il crevare
Et mori de suo amillo? Juro. Juro.

Molière laughs his quiet laugh.

AS LOUIS For it is this idea of myself, my essence you understand, that I wish to have carved in marble.

There is a roar, a shriek, of excruciating pain from Brutus.

AS LOUIS This will be my legacy to history.
AS BERNINI It will be very inconvenient for you, Sire, as I will require, a bust is so difficult, need, twenty-five sittings of three hours each.

Our Louis seems somewhat appalled. He rests his hand on the jeweled hilt of his sword, his other hand languishing on the knob of his cane.

AS LOUIS [*Long pause*] Oh. [*Long pause*] So much time?
AS BERNINI How else can history be achieved?
AS LOUIS I will speak to Bellefonds. Rest assured, *Monsieur,* your absolute mastery is incontestable, especially in France. You are not appreciated half as much in Rome.
AS BERNINI [*Pause*] Perhaps it is as you say, Majesty.
AS LOUIS I suspect that it is. What will you do? How will you start? Tell me.
AS BERNINI It will be very difficult to capture in stone your long eyelashes.

AS LOUIS Ah.

⊙

He draws the royal head, full face and profile.

AS BERNINI To steep oneself in the likeness I must study you not in fixed pose but as you move normally about your daily business. I make many rapid sketches for the liveliness. The best moments are when someone has just finished speaking. Or is about to.

AS LOUIS One tires so quickly. I will not be speaking today. On another occasion perhaps.

With that *mon* Louis leaves and so do many others. The *Cavaliere* seems disappointed. I tell him that the King will have his way. The vast scope of his desires is common currency. They all require his constant attention.

⊙

I spend all my afternoons with Her of late in the gardens amid the lime trees the hyacinths the wisteria. Still, at least She sees me.

⊙

The *Cavaliere* and I are invited to eat at the King's table. An opportunity for me. In our honour the Queen is in attendance and *Madame La Princesse.* The Prince de Condé, silent, watchful, remains at the Queen's elbow.

Four courses of different soups, pickled starling tongues, a red *Chateau Buzey* from Provençe, some fruit.

AS BERNINI I adore raw fruit. Often it is all that I eat.

AS MADAME LA PRINCESSE Fruit fruit fruit. Is there not more to life than that, Italian Gentleman? It must be difficult for you here in France. Wouldn't you agree, Louis?, language food wine.

AS LOUIS Or so one would imagine.

A whole partridge stuffed with truffles.

AS BERNINI There is a foreignness here, yes, that is familiar to the artist. I am used to it. It is all familiar and falsely complex.

AS LOUIS What? But life here in France is quite simple.

AS BERNINI Can that be true?

AS LOUIS Do you doubt it?

COURTIER Perhaps what the *Cavaliere* means is that life is other than what we would believe it to be.

The Marquis de Bellefonds is quick to notice and whispers to me.

AS BELLEFONDS And now you speak for him?

A quantity of salad.

AS BERNINI The disappointment of expectations makes us foreign to our own universe.

AS LOUIS Where would we be if the *Cavaliere* had not come to visit us?

The Queen smiles.

The Marquis de Bellefonds asks after the French artists who work in Rome.

AS BERNINI There are two or three perhaps very competent French sculptors. I seem also to remember a painter.

AS BELLEFONDS And who are they?

AS BERNINI I cannot for the moment recall their names.

AS BELLEFONDS And how is this portrait to be, *Cavaliere*?

AS BERNINI *Sì sì*. How do we capture the complexion of a face with merely monochromic marble? So, it is necessary to represent features in marble as they cannot possibly exist. The eyes, we must hollow them out to achieve these missing effects of colour. In the end we have what? A symbolic portrait of a great leader.

AS LOUIS Good. Very good. Very very good.

Some mutton and ham.

AS BERNINI I will do the best I can, Sire. Even the great and divine Michelangelo was never willing to undertake portrait sculpture.

Salmon *meunière* with dill *à la Flavigny.*

AS BERNINI *Grato m'è il sonno, e più d'esser di sasso;*
   Però non mi destar; deh! parla basso.
AS MADAME LA PRINCESSE And this means exactly?
COURTIER "Sleep is long and loved like a stone...."

The Queen, luminous, gently touches her brow.

AS QUEEN Allow me, *Monsieur,* to translate.
   "Deep to me is sleep, more dear to me but stone;
   Then wake me not; speak in an undertone."
   Is not the Italian so beautiful.
AS LOUIS Ah, very subtle.
AS QUEEN Like music. You should learn more Italian, *mon* Louis, out of respect for our guest.
AS LOUIS Only if I can have you as a tutor, my dearest Marie-Thérèse.

A dish of pastry.

Her Majesty, smiling, says to me:

AS QUEEN How is it that you speak Italian?

COURTIER I traveled to Italy with my uncle. As a boy, Your Majesty, after the death of my father. I have only a little of it left but I try to make myself understood by *Cavaliere* Bernini so as to attend to his needs.

AS LOUIS And his ideas, you find them interesting?

I hesitate. No one answer seems best.

AS MADAME LA PRINCESSE He praises very little here, Louis.

COURTIER He also finds few faults, Sire.

AS QUEEN He sees nothing worthy of praise because he has been so very hard at work on your portrait since his arrival in France.

AS LOUIS This is most unfortunate.

The King turns to me.

AS LOUIS Let him see the country.

A last course, that of compotes and preserves, is brought in. I feel that the moment of departure has suddenly passed.

AS LOUIS The Isle de France. Rochefort-en-Yvelines, where the great cutting runs through the woodlands rolling to the farthest western horizon. Chérence and the renowned pair of oaks, so perfect in the spring. Wy-dit-Jolivillage, simply perfect. Montgeroult. It has always been the same, and will always be so. I adore the outdoors. I tell you I think nothing of riding from Paris to Fontainebleau or hunting wolf deep into the darkest night.

AS BELLEFONDS His Majesty once killed nine wolves in a single day. LaRoche could not believe the King's prowess.

AS LOUIS You must come hunting with us, Monsieur Barnani.

The *Cavaliere* whispers to me:

AS BERNINI It is Bernini.

AS LOUIS Come. We will go to Fontainebleau tomorrow after mass.

COURTIER I'm not sure that the *Cavaliere* would really like it.

The table is now littered with dishes. The King picks at a carcass.

AS LOUIS That is most disappointing, Monsieur. Most disappointing.

⊙

We visit the cabinet meeting at Saint-Germain. Affairs of state are conducted as the King plays tennis with the Chevalier de Nogent. The *Cavaliere* draws with intense concentration. How peculiar he is.

AS LOUIS I was on the point of dining with my brother, the Duc d'Orléans.

The Marquis de Bellefonds turns to the King.

AS BELLEFONDS Then I fear you would not have eaten especially well.

AS LOUIS Still there are other attractions.

They all laugh knowingly. The spirits are high. Bernini banters and exchanges gallantries with *mon* Louis.

AS BERNINI *Sto rubando.*

COURTIER "… I am taking something from you."

Mon Louis, eloquent as always, replies in Italian, much to the admiration of the cabinet:

AS LOUIS *Sì ma è per restituire.*

COURTIER "… Yes, but it is only to give it back."

AS BERNINI *Però per restituir meno del rubato.*

COURTIER "… I give back less than I take."

The cabinet buzzes over the meaning of this exchange. It bodes well. I now feel pleased that I am with Bernini. Their game resumes. Its particular sound. Is it a snap, a ping?

Suddenly and unexpectedly the *Cavaliere* arranges the King's hair to suit himself. All are silent.

AS LOUIS As you wish, *Monsieur* Burnned.

The Prince de Condé, slowly limping across the wide space.
In a quiet voice he speaks briefly into the royal ear and then
slowly, leaves. The Queen arrives, she is brittle, there are
whispers of war. She seats herself with *Madame La Princesse*
while the *Cavaliere,* on his knees upon the floor, draws the
King. Bernini seems overjoyed at the Queen's visit. They
speak briefly in Italian. Suddenly he is different, more
subtle. I have never seen anyone like this before.

AS BERNINI Madame, your presence overwhelms me....
COURTIER Remember the bow, *Cavaliere.*

The Queen stops me with a gentle motion of her hand.

AS QUEEN I knew the *Cavaliere,* the Maestro, in *Roma....*

The Queen turns to *mon* Louis.

AS QUEEN May I speak with you, Louis, as soon as the
    Cavaliere has finished his work for the day?
AS LOUIS But of course, my dear Marie-Thérèse. I am always
    available to you.

Her smile is so radiant.

AS QUEEN Thank you, Sire.

With that exchange the Queen leaves and *Madame La Princesse* with her. The Marquis de Bellefonds whispers in the royal ear, and momentarily *mon* Louis tells the *Cavaliere* he too must go....

AS LOUIS ... But I will return whenever I am needed.

⊙

I spend all my afternoons with Her of late in the gardens amid the lime trees the hyacinths the wisteria.

COURTIER Perhaps tomorrow I will be able to present you to Signor Bernini.
AS SAINT-CHRISTOPHE I have already met your *Cavaliere.*
COURTIER Who has introduced you? The Chevalier de Nogent?
AS SAINT-CHRISTOPHE How funny you are!

She smiles and turns away from me.

⊙

At the Hôtel de Frontenac, *mon* Louis is here before me. The Marquis de Bellefonds is with him, as is the Prince de Condé, and forty or fifty others. All is abuzz. The Chevalier de Nogent arrives, splendid in a blue damask jacket, to much applause, and joins his father. There is a great press in the room. Almost unpleasant. So many perfumes and waters. The *Cavaliere* smiles when he sees me.

AS BERNINI Ah, a familiar face. These people it is like an army.

The King has brought several of his favourite hounds. The animals growl and bare their fangs. I pray for just one more day on this earth! Surrounded by these large animals *mon* Louis rests his hand on the jeweled hilt of his sword the other as always on the knob of his cane.

AS LOUIS And so?
AS BERNINI It is time to see what the stone will tell us.

The *Cavaliere* begins to work directly on the marble. Wooden mallet on steel chisel. The ringing never seems to stop.

Mon Louis asks the Marquis de Bellefonds in a whisper all can hear if his nose is really so misshapen.

Laughter.

AS BELLEFONDS Pray consider His Majesty's passion for symmetry, *Monsieur.*
AS BERNINI The King's mouth and nose are far from classically perfect. Look. The nose is narrower at the cheeks than at the top. This I faithfully represent. Look here, one side of the nose is wider than the other.

Silence.

AS BERNINI The marble is turning out better than I expected. But I must take the greatest of care with it. It is so *delicato,* "delicate" you understand.

Mon Louis does not banter with the *Cavaliere.* The King leaves and so does everyone with him.

COURTIER The King is very sensitive about his nose.
AS BERNINI Of course, who isn't?
COURTIER But he is the King.
AS BERNINI Kings popes, they all have noses. Please beg the Marquis de Bellefonds on my behalf to ask His Majesty that henceforth I will need a more regular schedule for the sittings. And a smaller army perhaps? Can you do that for me? Can you? No one else will help me.
COURTIER I will try.
AS BERNINI The days are long now. The light is too good to waste. I have asked for, was promised, twenty-five sittings of three hours each. Three hours. I need this time with the King. Ah, Cardinal Barberini said I would die on this journey. Perhaps he was right.

I speak to the Marquis de Bellefonds at the King's *levée*

COURTIER I fear that the *Cavaliere* will be put off by the slowness of the work.

AS BELLEFONDS These Italians. It must be their abominable cuisine.

Mon Louis, the sun of the world, overhears us:

AS LOUIS I do not care. I will not sit for anyone if and when I do not wish it. You would be wise to keep him under control.

⊙

The early summer is upon us gratefully upon us.

Cardinal Antonio Barberini comes often to see him. The whispers at court tell me that the Cardinal's presence is too often noticed. And mine with them. The King sends word that he will not now be available until further notice. I begin to fear now for the *Cavaliere's* safety. It can all become quickly unfortunate. I remember Pierre Claude-Marie LaRoche.

⊙

An early morning. The Chevalier de Nogent and... and *Mademoiselle* de Saint-Christophe arrive. It is She, my heart. We do not speak in the public view, She and I, but but it is so painful to have agreed to this. The whispers now say She loves another. She murmurs to the Chevalier de Nogent, and they laugh.

Mademoiselle de Saint-Christophe admires the fine bearing of the portrait.

AS BERNINI The pose is so natural to His Majesty that every time he comes, infrequent as it is, he assumes his place in exactly the same manner.
AS SAINT-CHRISTOPHE I am reminded of the head of Jupiter.
COURTIER Exactly right, *Mademoiselle.*

The Chevalier de Nogent asks of the stubble.

COURTIER Stubble, my dear *Chevalier?* You speak of stubble?
AS BERNINI No no. A man's face only remains smooth for two maybe three hours after shaving. Therefore some stubble should be hinted at. It is correct.

Cardinal Antonio Barberini arrives and reads a poem in Italian he has received from Rome. I do not quite understand all the words. Is that a quiet sneer from the Chevalier de Nogent?

AS BERNINI It is a request for me not to do this bust.
COURTIER But why?

AS BERNINI Why? Why? Because what's the point of remaining in Paris when there can only be one Louis. It is nothing but flattery.

COURTIER From whom is this poem?

AS CARDINAL BARBERINI Pope Innocenzo.

She is impressed.

AS CARDINAL BARBERINI The Holy Father has come to appreciate the superlative artistry of *Cavaliere* Gianlorenzo Bernini.

Surely now the *Cavaliere* will leave Paris. Will I now lose my apartment in Versailles?

AS CARDINAL BARBERINI He would like nothing more than for you to return to *Roma,* Gianlorenzo.

AS BERNINI Ah really?

AS CARDINAL BARBERINI Bellefonds believes only in French art for the French by the French.

AS BERNINI He has been prejudiced against me from the first. I know this.

AS CARDINAL BARBERINI Exactly my point.

AS BERNINI No no, I am here. And as I am here, let us for once dispense with the services of this Bellefonds.

COURTIER You may have only one enemy in Paris but be warned he is a great and powerful one.

Ma Saint-Christophe and the Chevalier de Nogent, oblivious to the ongoing conversation, giggle and whisper to each other.

AS CARDINAL BARBERINI Come back with me to *Roma*.

AS BERNINI No, I stay here but I am unimpressed by everything. Everything. Paris. Oh I hope I do not offend you.

COURTIER One is never advised to bypass the Marquis de Bellefonds.

AS BERNINI See what I must put up with? Bypass bypass. In *Italiano* we do not ever say "bypass." The word does not even fit into our language. I tell you it has all become so unpleasant. This Bellefonds, I have come to dislike and despise.

A vicious whispering campaign starts against Bernini. These weary crowds in Versailles milling milling the lackeys gossip soldiers smiles princes. Chaos barely controlled. I despair. Where is my little Molière? *"De remediis aucunis.... Juro. Juro."* Only he can make me smile and free me even if for a moment from this ceaseless restless passionately relentless pain in my darkest night heart. I know the whispers cannot be true.

As the *Cavaliere* takes his siesta as is the Roman custom, I go to the atelier where I find the Marquis de Bellefonds, together with *Mademoiselle* de Saint-Christophe, dressed exquisitely in blue taffeta and gray silk. She. They are accompanied by a platoon of musketeers, who take possession of the doors.

AS BELLEFONDS *Mon* Louis, the father of all brothers, is coming. You are to alert the Italian.

Bernini hurriedly dresses. The Queen is announced by the Prince de Condé. The Marquis de Bellefonds seems, for once, disconcerted. All bow to Her Majesty, *Mademoiselle* de Saint-Christophe the lowest. The Queen, with a gracious nod and a smile to the *Cavaliere,* immediately turns and leaves. A hush. *Ma* Saint-Christophe is greatly embarrassed as the whispers start.

AS BERNINI I am truly sorry the Queen could not stay. She is the voice of reason.
AS BELLEFONDS I am certain you are right, *Monsieur* Berninu.

I put my hand on his arm.

AS BERNINI It is Bernini.
AS WARIN And a well-admired name it is, *Monsieur.*

The artist, *Monsieur* Warin, a man much respected, a member of the Academy. Everyone eagerly awaits his opinion.

AS WARIN I think that the great Maestro has taken too much off the forehead and what is taken from the marble cannot be put back.

AS BELLEFONDS I think mostly that if we were to move the bust, say to Versailles, *mon* Louis would therefore have less farther to come for these sittings of yours.

AS BERNINI But that is exactly the issue. Why is the King not more available?

There is no response.

AS BERNINI Where are my chisels? Where are my chisels?

Irritated, the *Cavaliere* leaves. In heavy silence we wait. [*Pause*] The Chevalier de Nogent appears, splendid in his blue damask jacket, and seems surprised that the King is not here. He confers with his father, the Prince de Condé and with the Marquis de Bellefonds. Then the Prince de Condé and the Chevalier de Nogent have a brief heated discussion.

⊙

The King arrives, two hours later, alone, with the hounds. Gripping the jeweled hilt of his sword his fingers tapping on the knob of his cane, *mon* Louis scans the atelier, searching....

AS LOUIS Where is....?
COURTIER He will not come out because of the hounds.
AS LOUIS We grow so tired of the Italian.

The King sees *Mademoiselle* de Saint-Christophe and smiles.

I finally persuade Bernini to reappear.

COURTIER The King is in a mood, *Cavaliere.* Be gentle with him.
AS BERNINI I am also in a mood. Who will be gentle with me?
AS LOUIS I am displeased at the amount of dust in the atelier.

The *Cavaliere* is covered in it.

Ma Saint-Christophe and the Marquis de Bellefonds speak in an animated fashion, the Chevalier de Nogent bristles, which makes those assembled whisper that the matter is of no small import. I cannot think what She wants. They all ignore the *Cavaliere.* The Prince de Condé stares at me with his hooded eyes.

The Prince de Condé whispers something in the royal right ear. The Marquis de Bellefonds whispers something in the royal left ear.

AS BERNINI Sire, we must make the most of what is fine and give the whole an effect of grandeur minimizing what is ugly....

AS LOUIS Are you suggesting, *Monsieur,* that....

AS BERNINI Your eye sockets are big but the eyes themselves are small and appear somewhat dead and that you hardly ever open them wide, you understand, contributes to a drooping shifty look.

Bated breath.

AS BERNINI *Sì sì va bene.* Thus I make them larger and thus we achieve the desired royal gaze, nobleness and grandeur befitting of a great Monarch.

AS LOUIS I am glad to hear that, *Monsieur.*

The Marquis de Bellefonds now speaks at length with *mon* Louis and returns to *ma* Saint-Christophe. I hate this secrecy.

Ma Saint-Christophe then speaks to *mon* Louis at great length. The King listens most attentively. *Ma* Saint-Christophe.... Oh I hope She will be discrete. [*Pause*] Or do I? All the while the *Cavaliere* attempts to show himself to the royal gaze. Molière could not have written a better farce. I look away. The Prince de Condé slowly leaves.

AS BERNINI Majesty, have the goodness to remain *immobile*. We are at a most significant part.

A secret cruel smile across the crowded room.

AS BERNINI Majesty, observe how some locks of hair show through the others. A most difficult thing to do.

The King looks intensely at *Mademoiselle* de Saint-Christophe. The Chevalier de Nogent tramps out. The King turns to the *Cavaliere*.

AS LOUIS I will be leaving.
AS BERNINI No, I need you here.
AS LOUIS What?
AS BERNINI It is imperative, Sire, that at this moment I have your complete and absolute attention.
AS LOUIS Can you not use all those drawings you have made, *Signor* Barnani? After all there are simply scads of them.
AS BERNINI Bernini, Sire, it is Bernini.
AS LOUIS Yes, precisely.
AS BERNINI These drawings are merely to soak and impregnate me with your image. To use these drawings for the portrait would be to make a copy instead of an original.

AS LOUIS I will not return tomorrow.

AS BERNINI I am Bernini.

AS LOUIS I will not be able to come for some time.

AS BERNINI An artist to whom even a Pope has deferred.

AS LOUIS *Je suis désolé mais le pouvoir des rois est absolu.*

AS BERNINI It is my own death. My own death.

AS LOUIS What did he say? I do not understand. Where is Bellefonds? Where is Bellefonds?

AS BELLEFONDS Sire?

AS LOUIS Attend me now.

The King leaves. They all leave.

The *Cavaliere* throws himself into a chair and puts his head between his hands. He remains thus for a considerable time.

AS BERNINI I will leave France tomorrow. I will write on every door, every door, *Addio i Francesi addio Francesi. Francesi.* This marble is *troppo cotto.*

He kicks over the chair *mon* Louis, the ice of eternity, is accustomed to lean against whilst posing.

Ma Saint-Christophe prepares to leave. I take her arm. She resists but I refuse to let go.

COURTIER May I see you?

AS SAINT-CHRISTOPHE You have broken our one and only rule.

COURTIER No one is looking.

AS SAINT-CHRISTOPHE They are always looking.

COURTIER May I see you?

AS SAINT-CHRISTOPHE I will write.

COURTIER When?

AS SAINT-CHRISTOPHE When I can.

COURTIER When?

AS SAINT-CHRISTOPHE When I can.

She pulls her arm free from my grasp.

End of Act

Act Two

COURTIER: Most days now I stay to eat with the *Cavaliere.*
Apricots are plentiful and early sweet melons. *E dolce bello.*

⊙

Many days pass in silence.

⊙

He lies in a darkened room with a cloth over his face.

COURTIER You should return to Rome.

⊙

When he can rouse himself from his lethargy these sad days,
late nights, he roams through the vast rooms of state.

⊙

We stroll the upper walks of the garden. The heavy perfume
of jasmine and sweet william and oleander envelopes us.
A solitary lark sings its sad song.

AS BERNINI There is no view.

I think to myself: this dark sky fills me. I am weary as again night comes to night and all is silhouette. This day and the next I will not be at home to anyone…. She will not write. I am a fool.

AS BERNINI Night comes to night. And all is death.

⊙

The Marquis de Bellefonds arrives with a single musketeer. The Marquis has killed the Chevalier de Nogent in a duel. Blue jacket red blood. The Prince de Condé is in mourning. He now dresses only in black. The King is furious with the *Cavaliere* and has refused to see him. I remember the hunt at Fontainebleau… and my vow.

After looking at the bust for a long while the Marquis de Bellefonds says:

AS BELLEFONDS I would only wish that *Signor* Bernona had put more hair on the forehead.
AS BERNINI Bernini. Try to say it. Bernini Bernini, Gianlorenzo Bernini.
AS BELLEFONDS Bernini. Bernini.
AS BERNINI Bernini. The King has a forehead of great beauty. It should not be covered up.
AS BELLEFONDS But *mon* Louis, the mirror of my soul, does not any longer wear his hair in this fashion.
AS BERNINI What does it matter?

AS BELLEFONDS What matters more?

AS BERNINI It is necessary for this forehead to compensate for the limits of nature.

AS BELLEFONDS And what if this, this statue of yours, does not even does not even look like the King?

AS BERNINI No matter what, my King will last longer than yours.

AS BELLEFONDS Our beloved Louis is concerned.

AS BERNINI Then let him be concerned for that is then what I shall capture in stone.

AS BELLEFONDS By the way it is not necessary to move the work to Versailles.

COURTIER Why?

AS BELLEFONDS Why?

The Marquis regards me coldly. I should not have spoken.

AS BELLEFONDS Why? Because the court will be here in Paris for a week.

AS BERNINI Only a week?

AS BELLEFONDS Consider yourself fortunate to have that. Do you need anything else?

The Marquis goes without waiting for the *Cavaliere's* response. His soldier goes with him.

COURTIER I am ashamed at the way they treat you.

AS BERNINI I do not like this Bellefonds.

COURTIER These days I even fear for my own safety.

AS BERNINI But why?
COURTIER Because I am seen by some as your ally.
AS BERNINI And so you are.

Endlessly he adjusts the red chalk marks on the eyes.

AS BERNINI Look. Last evening I worked by torchlight to
adjust this lock of hair on the forehead. See how I have
carved it filigree-like one strand above the other. It is as
if they stand free.

The *Cavaliere* works on the hair with water and sandpaper.
Endlessly hour after hour after hour. He fills the great room
with a fine white powder.

AS BERNINI It is so difficult to work this marble.
COURTIER Excuse me, *Cavaliere.* [*He sneezes*] It is beautiful.
AS BERNINI I know I know it is the dust. And your fine
clothes.
COURTIER It is nothing.
AS BERNINI I see you trying to clean them when you think
I am not looking. This marble is too brittle. It is a mir-
acle that I have succeeded as well as I have.

It rains a cold summer rain. *Ma* Saint-Christophe appears. She sings a delightful... some Italian songs by Monteverdi.

AS SAINT-CHRISTOPHE I had hoped that this aria would please you in your sadness. But I can see that I have failed.

AS BERNINI *Ma no grazie, Signorina* de Saint-Christophe, *grazie tante.*

She looks away from me and to the portrait.

AS SAINT-CHRISTOPHE What are these red marks, *Cavaliere?*

AS BERNINI I mark the iris of the eyeball with red chalk. When the work is finished, I shall use the chisel like so to remove them and the resulting shadows will represent the pupils of the eyes which will then tell us everything.

The Prince de Condé, in black, and many others, in black, arrive. *Ma* Saint-Christophe withdraws to the shadows.

The *Cavaliere* works at the royal portrait from many perspectives. Many of the assembled begin to giggle at the great energy and strange postures Bernini assumes. The Marquis de Bellefonds and the Prince de Condé glare at each other. The *Cavaliere* notices nothing.

Ma Saint-Christophe now emerges from the shadows. The Marquis de Bellefonds appears at her side. *Ma* Saint-Christophe is not smiling. The Marquis de Bellefonds looks away from her.

AS BELLEFONDS What is wrong with the King's mouth?

Laughter.

AS BERNINI Nothing. It is a mouth. Useful I am sure for those things that the mouth is good for: talking eating spitting drinking kissing smiling frowning. Here I have chosen the moment when the King is about to speak.
AS BELLEFONDS The King has had enough of you and your noise and muck.
AS BERNINI I will need more sittings.
AS BELLEFONDS Do your job.

The Prince de Condé watches *ma* Saint-Christophe and the Marquis de Bellefonds as they have a heated whispered exchange. The Marquis de Bellefonds then storms out.

AS BERNINI What is happening?

The Prince de Condé watches *ma* Saint-Christophe.

AS BERNINI Is that the King I see in the corridor, waiting?
COURTIER Perhaps you are mistaken.

Ma Saint-Christophe leaves.

AS BERNINI Is that the King? Why is the King being kept from me?

COURTIER The King will have his way. The royal mind everywhere curious dangerous back and forth here and there. First begonias and then palm trees. Stags then hounds. Page boys, ladies! The King will have his way. His majesty has many appetites. They all require his constant attention. At moments like this, I pray. For most of us the merely momentary royal glance is what we crave. Is it missing for so much as a day?: there might be circumstances. Five days: perhaps it is true that the King desires my mistress. Eight days: we expect with trepidation to find the Marquis de Bellefonds at our door. Oh Lord, please grant me just one more day on this earth. I am very sympathetic to your position, *Cavaliere,* but it is highly unlikely.

I see now that all will elude me.

⊙

Cardinal Antonio Barberini and Molière sit silently by him. He has added only a single lock of hair to the forehead.

AS BERNINI This lock of hair is totally in deference to the views of the Marquis de Bellefonds who has been so kind as to point out to me on numerous numerous numerous occasions that the King never leaves his forehead uncovered. How was I to know? The French are so concerned about seeming dated in their fashion.

COURTIER I like it this way, for it shows the slight hollow in the middle of the forehead to a great advantage.

AS BERNINI *Grazie.* I am especially proud of this little curl here.

Molière joins us, speaking in his soft special way.

AS MOLIÈRE I congratulate you.

AS BERNINI But finally what does a piece of hair matter?

AS MOLIÈRE Exactly. The King, not his hair, is the story of this statue. And who is the narrator of the story? You, you *Cavaliere,* you are the narrator. It is you who tells us the story of this great King, a King who therefore becomes an actor in your play.

AS BERNINI *Sì,* as if a great facade. We stand back and contemplate it. *La facciata.* We move through parallel, flexible worlds becoming aware of niches ornamented with saintly shadows. Highlights emerge lurking in some forgotten past. The eye the heart is in motion constantly constantly in motion swirled and taken this way that way. False perspectives alarm and excite us. We are breathless

AS MOLIÈRE Ah, this audience becomes your instrument.

AS BERNINI *Sì sì,* but can this story ever be told, completely told?

AS MOLIÈRE But... the quest, *Monsieur.*

AS BERNINI *Sì sì.* I like your voice. An actor's voice. The gentle touch. The words continue though I cannot speak them. The words continue. I wish you spoke more Italian, *Signor* Molière.

After a pause Cardinal Antonio Barberini comments:

AS CARDINAL BARBERINI There is talk, idle talk I am sure, of actually destroying the portrait.

Tears in his eyes, Molière puts his hand on the *Cavaliere's* shoulder.

AS MOLIÈRE It can be a hard world, *Monsieur.*

⊙

The nights begin to be cool.

Nobody comes to see him. It is said of the *Cavaliere* in the court that he is remote and even a fraud.

AS BERNINI I must see the King as soon as possible, for we finish this face together, he and I. I am unable to truly work here in France. Ah, *Roma.* [*He Sighs*] So many mistakes in a life. I wish that the Queen would visit me. She is the voice of reason. Women are the source of my strength.

Is it because of *ma* Saint-Christophe that the Queen does not come to see him? In this I have failed him as well as myself.

He polishes the drapery.

AS BERNINI What do you think of it? I want it to look as... as... light as airy as possible. These lesser folds, undulations, emerge, so gentle from the broad surfaces only to disappear again with a most noble harmony and without concealing these most beautiful contours of the underlying structure.

COURTIER Like it is floating in the wind.

AS BERNINI See, the body moves with the drapery but I do not allow this whole left to right movement to continue unchecked. No. No no. This barrier on the right this mass of drapery curling slowly upward serves to bring it all to rest. [*Pause*] I am afraid all the time.

I happen again to meet the artist, *Monsieur* Warin, and take him to see the *Cavaliere,* hoping that this visit will cheer him.

AS WARIN I find the portrait striking in likeness but I feel the jaw is now too prominent. And the nose somewhat larger on one side....

AS BERNINI Again, the nose.

AS WARIN ... and narrower at the back, here, than in the front. Is it not more symmetrical in life?

AS BERNINI This is the way I see it. Most people think that the forehead goes back too far and is too hollow about the eyes. But be assured, the nose is the feature next most commented upon. Enough of this, enough. I am tired of it. All this chatter. Endless chatter. The noise of stupidity is loud in France and yours, *Monsieur* Warin, is the loudest. The loudest!

Monsieur Warin is very much alarmed.

AS WARIN Don't speak so....

AS BERNINI I will only accept criticism from someone more capable than myself, not from someone like you, *Monsieur* Warin, an artist not worthy to clean the soles of my shoes.

⊙

The *Cavaliere* remains extremely agitated. One moment he is going to the Marquis de Bellefonds the next to Cardinal Antonio Barberini the next he is returning to Rome the next he is destroying the career of *Monsieur* Warin. A veritable frenzy. My own father was like this before he died.

AS BERNINI I do not see why after all the contempt that has been shown me that I, myself, should not take a mallet to this piece of stone and destroy it. Better me than them.

A letter is brought to me. I cannot breathe.

COURTIER It is nothing. A dealer in marble.

After dinner I go to her apartments in the palace. She is not pleased to see me.

COURTIER The *Cavaliere's* bust is meeting with a somewhat chilly reception.
AS SAINT-CHRISTOPHE *Je suis désolé* but what can one do?
COURTIER Be careful.
AS SAINT-CHRISTOPHE In the future it would be best if you did not visit me unless requested to do so.
COURTIER Do you love me? [*Pause*] You are most cruel to me, *Madame.*
AS SAINT-CHRISTOPHE [*Pause*] You are seen too often here.
COURTIER Not often enough.
AS SAINT-CHRISTOPHE Please. For me.

His Majesty arrives accompanied by the Marquis de Bellefonds, and *Mademoiselle* de Saint-Christophe. The King is so witty and jovial. He smiles often at *ma* Saint-Christophe. She is demure. I notice that the others remain at the door not daring to come any further into the room. The whispers speak of a liaison in the King's bed. I say to all it cannot be true. It is not true! The whispers say the Queen is enraged. The King is infectious in his enthusiasm.

The *Cavaliere* works with great joy at the nose and at the small mark that the King has near the right eye. The King walks about from time to time inspecting the work, talking quietly with *Ma* Saint-Christophe, and then resuming his pose.

AS LOUIS Please tell the *Cavaliere* for me that I find the likeness more pleasing in its symmetry especially. And that I am beginning to appreciate somewhat my new large forehead.

They all agree.

AS LOUIS You must come hunting with me, *Cavaliere*. Tomorrow.

AS BERNINI I must work. I am so in love with this stone.

AS LOUIS Yes I understand your passion. Are you surprised? It is how I feel for the chase. And yet it all goes to ruin. Yesterday we roused a stag of ten tines; ran him for six hours; and on the point of taking him just as Bellefonds was about to sound the mort all the pack went off on the wrong scent in pursuit of a young brocket. Thus must I renounce the hounds as I have already relinquished the falcons. Ah, I am a most unhappy King.

COURTIER But there are yet a goodly number of falcons remaining, Sire.

AS LOUIS But who is to train them? LaRoche is dead, a tragic hunting mishap. I alone now must preserve the true art. With my passing all will be lost and the game will henceforth be taken only by snares pitfalls traps. As a favour to me, *Cavaliere,* to me personally, come with us to Fontainebleau tomorrow.

The Prince de Condé arrives and without ceremony approaches the King, whispers. The King glares at the Marquis de Bellefonds, who is again disconcerted. The King raises a hand to his eyes, and reaches tenderly towards *ma* Saint-Christophe.

I take the opportunity to speak in Italian to the *Cavaliere.* I care not now who hears us.

COURTIER I will come with you. I will break my vow to never again the chase. It will be your first hunt and my last.

AS LOUIS Then you'll come with us on the hunt, my dear *Cavaliere.*

COURTIER Do this. It is the only way you will ever get to finish the portrait.

Reluctant as he is to go, reluctant as I am to go, my argument is convincing and the arrangements are made.

⊙

That night against all that pride and reason tell me, my fear for She brings me to Her apartments, but there is no answer to my calls. Oh let me love You. I will protect You.

Again without response. An air of strangeness. I see Her everywhere emerging from every dark corridor. A cold wind. I see Her in the distance with who? With whom? Shadows. Too soon the dawn comes.

⊙

We leave to hunt early right after mass, the morning air so clear. One might have felt for a moment one could really see. The gentlemen of the court seem in fine fettle.

AS BERNINI These trees are so beautiful. What are they called?

COURTIER They are called elms.

AS BERNINI Ah. Elms. Elms. Now tell me why does the *Grand Dauphin* not accompany us? Such a handsome child.

COURTIER According to ancient ritual the *Grand Dauphin* is to be kept from absolutely everything.

AS BERNINI I do not understand.

The *Cavaliere* uses a *calèche* as befitting a Roman gentleman.

AS BERNINI I do not like this blood hunt.

COURTIER Nor I.

Pheasants are abundant and the King finds scarcely a moment to rest from his shooting. He is ecstatic. I have never seen him as happy.

AS LOUIS There, there, I have shot seven.

All applaud.

Madame La Princesse rides abreast of us on her dappled gray mare.

AS MADAME LA PRINCESSE Where is *Monsieur* LaRoche? He is so useful on these occasions.

Can it be she does not know?

AS LOUIS There, there, I have shot nine.

AS MADAME LA PRINCESSE Did you hear the scandal? The Duchesse du Guise? Her gambling losses are so heavy that the *Duc* has been forced to sell his family jewels. Not that they had much to begin with.

AS LOUIS There, did you see, there, I have shot twelve more.

AS MADAME LA PRINCESSE And have you not heard of *Mademoiselle* de Saint-Christophe?

My heart stops.

AS MADAME LA PRINCESSE Nothing but trouble that one. The little hussy. Found this morning floating in the Seine....

She leans towards us.

AS MADAME LA PRINCESSE ... naked I am told. Some say
  suicide but I prefer to think not.

The Marquis de Bellefonds rides by on Brutus.

AS BELLEFONDS I have heard she was a spy for the Pope.

Bellefonds avoids my glance.

AS MADAME LA PRINCESSE Good riddance to bad rubbish,
  don't you agree?

Brutus rears as they ride to join the King.

In the silence, a bird, suddenly so large, flies across the sky.

AS LOUIS There. There. Thirty-eight in all. Thirty-eight
  pheasants.
AS MADAME LA PRINCESSE Remarkable, Louis, truly remarkable.
AS LOUIS Is this not the life, *Cavaliere*?

I have no more words.

We sit in the *calèche*.

The *Cavaliere* searches the sky.

AS BERNINI Here, I am a strange blind bird. When I am
as I am now, but in *Roma* you understand, I am more
as if a *giardino magnifico,* overgrown and lush, a villa in
glorious ruin. I fill my stage with lilies a festival of myself,
and then I go out into the crowds. Their voice fills me.
[*Pause*] Instead of sky I once suggested space decorated
with a gold coffering filled with the most delicate rosettes
painted only in black and white. We are alone.

I turn and discover that the rest of the hunting party has
gone. The sun begins to go down, a breeze becomes a wind
and it is suddenly cool, even cold, in the approaching
autumn of my life.

The days become noticeably shorter. It is whispered that
there will now be war with the Netherlands. They do not
require Bernini's presence any longer.

The work on the portrait proceeds easily and well. Sometime
and perhaps soon it shall be over and I shall miss it more
than I can ever say. With whom will I speak Italian now?

He continues to work on the collar, minutely chiseling it out and disengaging it from the hair.

AS BERNINI Consider this....

The *Cavaliere* points out detail after detail after detail with which he is frustrated.

COURTIER But you are wrong. I have never seen anything like it before in my life. I will never see anything like it again.
AS BERNINI But you will. Every day there is a sunset. Your life is your own.
COURTIER I wish you were right.

We sit in silence.

COURTIER Expectations and disappointments.
AS BERNINI The disappointment of expectations makes us foreign to our own universe. Another battle. Another constant battle.

The court comes often. Controversy still continues but now Gianlorenzo seems to enjoy it and finds it most entertaining. There are many remarks concerning the collar. [*He mimics*] The French should not merely copy the ancient Romans. [*He mimics another voice*] The King should appear in the fashion of his time. [*He mimics another voice*] But do you think, it will surely be of interest to future historians? [*He mimics another voice*] Of course. Of course.

Her Majesty, the Queen, is announced by the Prince de Condé. She is radiant and magnanimous. The Queen bows very low to the *Cavaliere.* I am acknowledged.

The Queen says at once how perfect the portrait is. I can now understand their rapid Italian and they know this. They laugh, as if at a private jest, as if alone.

The Queen then reads the *Cavaliere* an Italian poem of her own devising:

AS QUEEN *Al signor Cavaliere* Bernini
  Qual sia più favorevole destino,
  Che trovat' il Bernini *habbia un Luigi,*
  O Luigi un Bernini.

A letter arrives from ma Saint-Christophe, mailed before her death. My hand shakes.

Her Majesty resumes:

AS QUEEN *Senza sì gran scultor foran sicuri*
  Non poter adorar il ver sembiante....

Her letter burns me to the touch.

The Queen glances towards me and I translate her poem for the assembled personages.

COURTIER "The question: is it more fortuned a destiny for Bernini to find Louis, or Louis, Bernini. Without so great a sculpture it is certain that future centuries would not be able to adore the true likeness of so great a King and no less true that there could not be throughout the world a subject better meriting his chisel."

Her letter smiles. Our walks in the garden. I am sorry, She says. We live in difficult and dangerous times, but who cannot say this? Tell no one what has happened. I never will. Burn this. I already have.

The *Cavaliere,* laughing, turns to me:

AS BERNINI It is absurd but I will need more sittings. Can you not again, I am sorry to ask you this, can you not speak again to our Marquis de Bellefonds?

We laugh until tears stream down our faces. At that moment the Queen turns to me and says in Italian.

AS QUEEN I am sorry for your loss.

Foreign to my own universe.

⊙

There was never to be another sitting. We knew this of course. The portrait, in its lonely splendour, would be considered finished.

He looks quietly about him.

AS BERNINI Soon I will go home. There is the work on the colonnade of the Piazza de San Pietro. It is all that I have ever wanted to do. [*He sighs*] It never entirely satisfies me, my work. I am never content.
COURTIER Nor I.
AS BERNINI But hopeful.
COURTIER Not I.

He smiles.

AS BERNINI There are only the eyes remaining.

Finally, grandly, kindly even, the King arrives. It is whispered that he has spoken with the Queen at length. He joins her and they stand together. All is abuzz.

The portrait, draped round with scarlet velvet. One hand resting on the jeweled hilt of his sword the other barely stroking the knob of his cane, Louis studies it for some time and makes the others do the same. Everyone vies to praise it. Several poems are written. The royal favourite, of course, is by Molière.

AS MOLIÈRE *Mesdames, messieurs, attention, attention.*
Je vous en prie.
Louis jusques ici n'avait rien de semblable,
On en voit deux, grâce au Bernin,
Dont l'un est invincible, et l'autre inimitable.

Molière bows. Looking to the King, the *Cavaliere* instantly
replies.

AS BERNINI *Risposta del Cavaliere Bernini:*
Non per far di Ré sì grande appoggio degno.
Che de sostegno no è mestier chi sostiene il mondo....
COURTIER The artist replies: "There may never exist a portrait
worthy of this King. For consider, it is he, and he alone,
who holds the world." Would you say this was right,
Monsieur Molière?

Molière applauds and we bow to each other. And then he
to the *Cavaliere,* and then all to the King.

Midst fanfare the final cut of the pupils is done. Slowly
carefully deliberately magically wonderfully tenderly bril-
liantly joyously the red chalk is cut away and the soul is
revealed. And I understand the *Cavaliere* as I have never
understood anyone. The lime trees the hyacinths the wisteria. Everything speaks to me now.

AS BERNINI It is finished. I have worked on it with such love. I wish that it had been more perfect.

AS LOUIS Tell *Cavaliere* Bernini that if only I had been able to understand his language, I would be able to convey my deepest feelings to him and say many things that should make him very happy and reveal to him how warmly I return his affection and how much I have come to value his presence here.

All applaud. Bernini is overwhelmed and cannot speak. He weeps and is gone. Louis is visibly moved. The final word is that of the Marquis de Bellefonds who praises the portrait till the heavens and bows to me, which makes me think that *mon* Louis, the voice of my past, truly admires it.

⊙

That night, we are alone in the vast and now empty Hôtel de Frontenac, the fire blazing against the mist and chill. A letter burns.

AS BERNINI The work completed becomes soon forgotten.

COURTIER But no. Through its eyes, which become my eyes, I have discovered for the first time, myself.

We look at the bust with the aid of a single candle.

COURTIER It is wonderful, Maestro.

AS BERNINI *Grazie grazie,* but it is always necessary to keep reminding myself that I have ever done anything.

COURTIER You have come to France and survived. Not all can say this.

AS BERNINI It comes to nought. If anything justifies a foolish man it is the pains he takes to discover his own importance.

COURTIER I will miss you.

AS BERNINI *Grazie tante.*

He bows perfectly to me.

AS BERNINI You see, I remember everything.

With that he left Paris, never to return.

⊙

Dark night late night. I drink a glass of my finest cognac in toast to the *Cavaliere* and another to Pierre Claude-Marie LaRoche and and yet another to the memory of a love I once had, a dream I once lived. To those who have gone as I never will, my spirit goes with them. And soon? And soon? [*Pause*] Oh Lord, please grant me just one more day on this earth. A silence. A long silence. Soon I will sleep and soon I will be happy. [*Pause*] Tears.

End of Play

Words in Italian, Words in French, a Recipe, and Two Poems

19 Salmon *meunière* with dill *à la Flavigny:*
Salmon rolled in flour and fried in butter, chopped
dill sprinkled on top, as eaten and enjoyed in
Flavigny, France.

36 *Je suis désolé mais le pouvoir des rois est absolu:*
I am sorry but the power of kings is absolute.

36 *Addio i Francesi:* Good-bye forever to the French

36 *Troppo cotto:* Overripe

39 *E dolce bello:* A beautiful sweetness

53 *Calèche:* An open carriage

56 *Giardino magnifico:* A magnificent formal garden

61 *Mesdames, messieurs, attention, attention.*
Je vous en prie.:
Ladies and gentlemen, your kind attention please.

61 *Louis jusques ici n'avait rien de semblable,*
On en voit deux, grâce au Bernin,
Dont l'un est invincible, et l'autre inimitable.:
Until this moment, our Louis was O so unique,
And yet now, because of Bernini, there are two,
One invincible, and the other, inimitable.

Production History

Through the Eyes was premiered by Nightswimming Theatre at the Theatre Center West in Toronto, October 1995, Naomi Campbell, producer.

with Julian Richings
directed by Brian Quirt
design by Dany Lyne
lighting by Bonnie Beecher
stage management by Naomi Campbell

Through the Eyes was produced by Factory Theatre in Toronto, January and February, 2003.

with Richard McMillan*
directed by Brian Quirt
design by Carolyn M. Smith
lighting by Paul Mathiesen
stage management by Kathryn Westoll

---

* In 2003, Mr. McMillan won the Dora Mavor Moore Award, Outstanding Performance by a Male in a Principal Role, for his performance in this production.

This production of *Through the Eyes* was remounted at Factory Theatre in May 2004, with Richard McMillan reprising his role. It was then toured to the Magnetic North Theatre Festival in Edmonton, June 2004, and the Thousand Island Playhouse in Gananoque, Ontario, July 2004.

Inquiries concerning production of this
play should be directed to the playwright:
113 Arthur Street South,
Elmira, Ontario,
Canada N3B 2N8
ddjb@golden.net

Don Druick is a distinguished playwright, a baroque flautist, and an avid herb gardener. His plays and translations have been frequently produced on stage and radio throughout Canada, and in Europe, Japan, and the USA.

Having lived in Vancouver and Montreal, Don Druick currently lives with artist Jane Buyers in Elmira Ontario, a small village 125 km west of Toronto.

Don Druick's previous works include the award-winning play *Where is Kabuki?* and the hit CBC radio series *Recipe for Murder.* He is presently working on *Tulip,* a dark play about the tulip trade in Holland in the seventeenth century, commissioned by Nightswimming Theatre.